Maryam Al Mansoori is an Emirati student from Ras Al-Khaimah studying at New York University Abu Dhabi. She spends most of her time contemplating about her life issues and goals. She is scared of cats but finds them cute. She loves sleeping, dark chocolate and walking. She is a supportive friend, a loving sister, a caring daughter and an independent woman.

To my parents who supported my work.

Maryam Al Mansoori

YOU ARE NOT ALONE

AUSTIN MACAULEY PUBLISHERS™
LONDON • CAMBRIDGE • NEW YORK • SHARJAH

ISBN – 9789948802518 – (Paperback)
ISBN – 9789948802525 – (E-Book)

Application Number: MC-10-01-1312495
Age Classification: E

First Published 2023
AUSTIN MACAULEY PUBLISHERS FZE
Sharjah Publishing City
P.O Box [519201]
Sharjah, UAE
www.austinmacauley.ae
+971 655 95 202

Throughout my journey of composing poems, I had people who gave me feedback or simply admired my work. My friends Shamma Al Khoori, Aisha Al Naqbi, Ali Al Dhaheri, Janine Micahella, Imane Larhlimi, Budoor, Safeya Alblooshi, Dania Hesham, Kacper Madejek, Daniyar Bolysbayev, Fatema Alrahbi, Maryam Alshehhi, Maryam Khalili, Se Young Park, and Yusril Nur Hidayat. Also, my aunt, Nora Abdulla and cousin, Shouq Fahad.

Table of Contents

Poet's Manifesto   **11**

Relationships   **13**

Screen Lover   *15*

Close and Distanced   *16*

Silent Moments   *17*

My Old Vitamin-D   *18*

Not a Game   *19*

Journey of Life   *20*

Not About Strangers   *22*

Your Shining Star   *24*

Friendship   *25*

Far Away   *26*

My Dear   *27*

Feelings   **29**

Hurt   *31*

Going Deep   *32*

The Pain of Memory   *34*

A New Experience   *36*

How Beautiful	38

Hidden Truth	39

Look at Her	40

Me Sometimes	41

Mental Health	**43**

The Abnormal	45

A Fantasy	46

Tooktalk	47

Icy Feeling	48

A Spirit Encounter	49

Broken Men	50

The Sound of Nature and Nurture	52

Let It Be	53

A Real Dream	54

Disturbed	55

Shallow	57

Courage	58

Pearl Rotana	59

Purpose	60

Poet's Manifesto

When I was an insecure child, hearing: *Maryam, Alreem, Sheikhat Al-hareem* from my Aunts always made me feel powerful. The phrase means Maryam, the gazelle, the queen of women. I chose Alreem as my poet name because it makes me feel empowered. Hence, it gives me the ability to make my readers feel the same way. I started with writing poems as a healing tool in 2019, but it grew to be my passion. So often, I am concerned with topics related to social expectations based on gender, suppression, fears, problematic idealism, toxic childhood programming, relationships, and anything about mental health. These concerns stem from my own experiences and circumstances.

Being an Arab and a Muslim woman, people – strangers, family members, and friends – have expectations for me. As a child, I thought that boundaries are identified universally based on who we are, when in reality, it was more about: what we are and who do we choose to be. In school, I didn't have to identify my personal boundaries when it came to relationships with the opposite gender. I studied in a segregated system hence, studying at NYUAD has been and *still is* a challenge for me. I had to learn about myself; my preferences, my concerns and my passions the hard way: I had to experience to decide what's right for me in terms of both academic and social life. For a long time, I hated myself. Media convinced me that I was inferior because of my language and my preferences. English, as a language, is valued more than Arabic. Hence, anything associated with the word English is also valued. Literature and Creative Writing major is considered a futureless path in my culture; engineering and medicine are the noblest choices. I thought that this sense of inferiority is inevitable, but it's not.

When I entered NYUAD, I met new people. I had non-local friends who valued me because of who I am. They admired and respected my language, culture, religion, and personality. I never thought this would happen, but it did. I started to love who I am and decided to never change for anyone but myself. Having such friends who valued me came with challenges too. Especially, the male ones. Most of them questioned my boundaries all the time out of concern by saying: "Are you okay with this?" Internally, I would say: "I don't know." Externally, I would say: "Yeah, I guess." Over time, instead of feeling inferior, I decided to feel unique by approaching my concerns with curiosity. I cry out without shame when I am in pain, but then I reflect, I journal and then compose poems.

This is me. This is Maryam Al Mansoori but you can call me Maryam Alreem *Sheikhat Al-hareem.*

Relationships

A sunrise in the Umm Al-Quwain's Desert

Screen Lover

In the corner of my screen,
It's staring with loving eyes,
Behind the curtains of the sheen,
It's waiting with fine lies.

In the corner of my screen,
It's searching in my eyes,
Behind the shields of the keen,
It's longing to rise.

In the corner of my screen,
It's wondering about my eyes,
Behind the walls of the dean,
It's wishing for allies.

Do we ever get to contact our eyes?
No no no, not until everyone dies.

Close and Distanced

We look alike,
We talk alike,
They call us a family.

We live nearby,
We walk nearby,
They call us a family.

I always lie,
I always deny,
They call us a family.

I always escape,
I always fake,
They call us a family.

We are close,
We are distanced,
They still call us a family.

Silent Moments

In the moments of silence,
I can hear its sound.
Wait for me, I am coming,
Don't leave me alone.

In the moments of silence,
I can hear its voice.
Almost there, few more days,
Don't leave me alone.

In the moments of silence:
I can hear its sound;
I need some time, but not much,
Don't leave me alone.

In the moments of silence,
I can hear its voice.
You've been patient, but please,
Don't leave me alone.

In the moments of silence:
I can hear it saying;
Give me a chance please,
I *can't* bear, to live alone.

My Old Vitamin-D

She believed in me,
When I didn't believe in myself.
I am confident now
Because of her.

She believed in me,
Until I believed in myself.
Until she felt unneeded,
And so chose to leave.

She believed in me,
I believed in her.
I am supportive now
Because of her.

She believed in herself,
I believed in myself.
We became confident,
So we *both* chose to leave.

Not a Game

You know what disgusts me about some men? How they approach a woman to prove a point. They just want to see if they can win her. As if she's a game. They play it until they win and then—the game lose its attractiveness. It gets boring so they play another game; another woman.

Don't play us. We are not a game.

You know what disgusts me about some women? How they seek a man's attention to prove a point. They just want to see if they can win him. As if he's a game. They play it until they win and then—the game lose its attractiveness. It gets boring so they play another game; another man.

Don't play us. We are not a game.

Instead, approach: you. Understand: you. Why prove a point? Aren't you good enough? You are: enough. You don't need: him or her to feel: good enough.
Self-love comes from within; he or she is there: your: company not complete.
When you play him or her, you're playing: you. Hurting: you. Feeding: you—with you being: toxic—to you.
So, no more gaming on people, because, we are; you're, not a game.

Journey of Life

Life is a journey for you to learn,
No matter how you feel,
It will take away the pain.

It's a journey of making mistakes,
Helps you learn from things you give,
And things you take.

Life is full of many lessons,
For those who see,
And are able to listen.

It's a journey that might feel as a cage,
But with insistence,
It will be easy to break.

Life is someone who can be your mate,
But not in your favor,
If you chose to hate.

During this journey you will meet friends,
For a long or a short time,
It depends.

People you might love and,
People you might hate,
Relatives, neighbors and classmates.

You will miss things that you will get,
Keep trying then,
You won't regret.

Life will take us through downs and ups,
If you're smart,
You will never give up.

Not About Strangers

We climbed the frozen mountain,
Me and other strangers.
We fought the avalanche—
Until we reached the top,
Everyone was relieved and happy,
In the top shelter,
Except for me.
For some reason that top made me,
A prisoner.
A prisoner of collective expectations,
Set by those strangers.
After all the suffering we went together,
I thought about going down that mountain,
To start over.
I was waiting for someone,
To support my decision.
But they all looked at me like I was a lunatic,
So I knew I had to do it alone.
I searched the top shelter,
For the exit door.
But instead I bumped to walls of,
Arts and sciences.
It felt as if I was trapped in a fancy maze,
But I continued searching,
Until I saw

That door of freedom.
I smiled, ran away,
Without hesitation or regrets,
To the bottom of the mountain.
Those strangers thought of me,
As a traitor.
So I had to disguise myself,
In a foreign outfit.
It was tough because I had to do it alone,
But you know what? I did it,
Because, it's not about strangers.

Your Shining Star

You smile every time you achieve your dreams,
You walk through the night questioning your means.
Can I be that someone who will achieve their dreams?
Suddenly a blurred vision and mind.

Among all this confusion someone leads you the way,
Words are powerful, they can open up your eyes and mind.
To reach what you aim by expecting what's given,
To open up your heart, and claim your needs.

Embrace your fears, embrace that person,
Show some love, care and interest.
That person is there for a good reason,
It's not a coincidence, it's meant to be,

To meet your shining star.

Friendship

You called it a friendship,
The day you met and,
Felt your veins and heartbeat.

You called it a friendship,
The time you laughed and shared,
Deep conversations and loving eyes.

You called it a friendship,
The days you suffered and asked,
For support and simply received it.

When you called it friendship,
Was it: an illusion? An excuse? An alternative?
Or just a glimpse of:
A hopeful future?

When you called it friendship,
Was it a dream?
Or because of fear,
A way to hide the truth?
How you really feel?
You called it a friendship,
With hopes for more,
Than: Friendship.

Far Away

Head in the clouds,
Every time you go away.
And you start to sway,
I go and find – you,
Beg you to be kind,
But it's all in my mind,
Not in the present,
Or in the heavens,
Just far away.

My Dear

Heal my dear,
Stay in bed,
Seal the deal,
Make sure you're fed,
I worry you'll be more sick,
I worry that the pain will kick,
So, stay covered in warmth, love and care,
Seal the matter with your affair,
Make sure you don't leave a trace,
Unless you want to start a case,
Against you for being a pain,
In my heart until I faint,
So stay in bed, a clone,
Heal my dear, alone,
Without me.

Feelings

The Cove Rotana Resort, Ras Al-Khaimah, UAE

Hurt

Fear of hurt; that cunning illusion; that thing that hurts. Are
you willing to take the risks? Is it worth it?
Yes, no. Sure, not sure. Brave, scared. All—fear of hurt.
What is it that you want? What matters to you the most?
Us—not getting hurt.

Going Deep

Going deep hurts.
It feels good at first.
But then—it hurts.

You get attached;
Letting them go gets hard;
If you do so someday then–
You're sad.

Because: going deep hurts.
Life feels so grey and dull;
You lose its meaning;
You feel lost;
You might even–
Lose yourself.

Because: going deep hurts.
You wonder if it was a mistake,
Being too vulnerable,
To someone who's meant to leave.
Sighs, sadness of nostalgia.
All to worry. And worry. And worry.
Because: going deep hurts.
Luckily, that's not always the case.

Luckily, some never leave;
They're meant to be here:
Forever. And ever. And ever.
Because: Going deep, sometimes, hurts.

Those sometimes are gems;
They appear briefly to make us
Stronger. Brighter. Wiser. Better—us.
Because: Going deep, sometimes, hurts—for a good reason.

The Pain of Memory

It's everlasting:
The sweetness and bitterness,
The talk and the walk;
Everything is leaving me with a smile,
And tearful eyes.

The eyes of the moon,
Curved on a rounded face,
Giving me the cute vibes,
Of mystery and misery.

We were different, yet
Similar, in the heart and mind.
Our timings matched,
They were like heavenly destined.
Made: to complete each other,
But then – left at last.

Sometimes, when I close my eyes,
I see it looking at me;
With a saddening smile.
I see it old in black, alone,
But doesn't dare to ask—
For company.
It only asks me to leave.

It only wants me to enjoy,
My days, my nights,
Move on, and leave it—
Alone, in the past.

35

A New Experience

Love is real,
Feeling of fear,
And mistreatment.

It makes you smile,
Talk comfortably,
And express feelings.

You share memories,
Listen to each other,
In all situations.

You crave care,
Meeting each other,
And long conversations.

Even with fear of
Judgments, you continue,
Accepting your feelings.

You might deny them,
When cultural conflict exists,
In this relationship.

You might mistreat,
Yourself and your—
Loving companion.

You might regret,
Complain, and blame yourself,
For embracing those feelings.

At the end, you learn,
Smiling after long nights,
Of crying and depression.

Choose to move on,
Stop that love, and start,
A new experience.

How Beautiful

How beautiful you are:
That you make me smile,
That you make me a fan—
Of everything about you.

How beautiful you are:
That you make me blush,
That you make me lush-
With everything about you.

How beautiful you are;
That you make me curious,
That you make me furious—
To know everything about you.

How beautiful you are:
That you make me happy,
That you make me sappy—
Because I like you.

Hidden Truth

My chest is heavy,
My eyes are dry,
My back is aching,
My brain is feeling high.

I cannot think straight,
I cannot look right,
I cannot fake strength,
I cannot anymore lie.

I am tired of all this show,
I am sick of this idealism,
I am tired of all this act,
I am sick of these lies.

So I screamed the truth.

My chest is light,
My eyes are wet,
My back is healed,
My brain is saying:
No more lies.

Look at Her

Look at her,
She seems smart,
She seems very independent.

Look at her,
She smiles a lot,
She seems very happy.

Look at her,
She studies in a decent place,
She must be very lucky.

Look at me,
Always unmotivated to study,
Always feeling lazy.

Look at me,
Feeling lost,
Feeling sick,
And uneasy.

Look at me,
Very unlucky but people—
See me differently.

Me Sometimes

Sometimes I feel like being rich is a
Crime.
Sometimes I feel like being relieved is
Unfair.
Sometimes I feel like being supportive is
Overrated.
Sometimes I feel like being smart is a
Flaw.
Sometimes I feel like being kind is
Unnecessary.
Sometimes I feel like being honest is
Condemned.
Sometimes I feel like being quiet is a
Pain.
Sometimes I feel like being alone is
Abnormal.
Sometimes I feel like being friendly is
Naïve.
Sometimes I feel like being happy is a
Mistake.
Sometimes I feel like being loyal is
Foolish.
Sometimes I feel like being strong is
Useless.

Sometimes I feel like being me is
Wrong.

42

Mental Health

Winter view from the library in NYUAD, Saadiyat Island

The Abnormal

Heads into the phone,
Gazes of loneliness.
Heads into the gazes,
Backs of loneliness.

Noise, noise, noise. Horn. Speeding cars. Annoyed heads.
Disturbing loneliness.

Heads into the laps,
Gazes of aliens.
Heads into the gazes;
Backs of aliens.

Silence, silence, silence. Wind. Streamed audios. Pleased
heads. Non-disturbing aliens.

Alone and happy or accompanied and lonely?
Alien and relaxed or native and disturbed?
The abnormal or the normal? I choose—the abnormal.

A Fantasy

Every night,
I lay down:
Imagining-my dreams,
Shaping-my future,
Telling-my fears,
Thinking of-my maneuver,
Rethinking—my mistakes,
Retelling—my past,
Reshaping—my aches,
Reimagining—my blast.

Every night,
I lay down living,
A fantasy.

Tooktalk

I took the train to my destination,
I was running,
I was late,
As usual.

I took the longest way,
I was hoping,
I was worrying,
As usual.

I took the path,
I was hesitant,
I was alone,
As usual.

I took me,
I was open,
I was hurt,
As usual.

I took,
I was,
I was,
As usual.

Icy Feeling

I lied down on ice,
Stared at the stars,
Sighed and thought about me.

I walked on ice,
Stared at my frozen feet,
Sighed and thought about the future me.

I played on ice,
Stared at my shaking hands,
Sighed and thought about the old me.

I lied down on ice,
Again, stared at the stars,
Sighed and thought about the present me.

This is life, freezes our warmth,
Until one night that warmth triumphs
the Icy feeling.

A Spirit Encounter

A spirit kissed my forehead,
Blew on me
When I was asleep.

A spirit patted my back,
Said, 'It's alright."
When I was asleep.

A spirit whispered in my ear;
Wake up now,
When I was asleep.

A spirit opened my eye lids;
Said, "It's time."
When I was asleep.

A spirit guarded my fleeting soul,
With care

When I was asleep.
A spirit made of me,
Had me
When I was asleep.

Broken Men

He's back, but broken.
Back with infected,
Red, and lost eyes,
Almost heartbroken.

I don't know what happened.
I'm scared to ask,
I fear to know the truth,
What made him broken.

His voice is shaky and slow,
As though dust lives in his throat,
Always dry, unable to talk,
Like someone internally broken.

His skin is darker; almost burned.
As though it was rubbed by stone,
Always ruff, unable to move,
Like someone externally broken.

My dear brother, tell me,
"How was it?"
"Not that bad," he said.
What a bad liar, I thought
While I'm left heartbroken.

It's okay if you cry,
You don't have to pretend or lie.
Tell me for real, how was it?
No response. Only sad eyes.

The Sound of Nature and Nurture

I go to morning walks to clear my mind,
I go without my headphones,
Just focusing on nature.
I hear the sound of birds, chickens, hammers and trucks,
I hear the sound of my sneakers rubbing the grass and floors.
All at once just like a song.

Clang clang sound of hammers gets louder,
Tweet tweet sound of birds gets lighter,
The sun becomes brighter, and
The neighborhood is more alive.

I go to night walks to clear my mind,
I go without my headphones,
Just focusing on nurture.
I hear the sound of blame, fears, dreams and thoughts,
I hear the sound of my sneakers rubbing the grass and floors.
All at once just like a song.

The hmmm sound of dreams gets louder,
The huf huf sound of blame gets lighter,
The moon becomes brighter, and
The neighborhood is more extinct.

Let It Be

Let it be on you sparkling,
The shines of pleasure along,
The darkness of misery.

Let it be on you sparkling,
The aura of transparency along,
The darkness of mystery.

Let it be on you sparkling,
The sense of satisfaction along,
The darkness of frustration.

Let it be on you sparkling,
The shines of perfections along,
The darkness of imperfections.

Let it be,
Yourself,
Let it be.

A Real Dream

I had a real dream,
About an angel,
Who checked up on me.

I had a real dream,
About someone who,
Cared for my feelings,
My thinking, and
My way of sleeping.

I had a real dream,
About something that,
Made me,
Forgive and love,
The real me.

I had a real dream,
That made me accept,
My reality.

Disturbed

The thing is:
I care too much,
That they start to not care.

I care too much,
Until I get disturbed annoyed and mad,
But you know what?
I'll no longer care.

Instead,
I'm gonna be this straight face bitch for those,
Who not care.

So what?
If they don't care.
It's actually for the best,
To invest on those,
Who care.

I'm too precious to be treated like nothing.
I'm too precious,
I'm too,
I'm so disturbed.
But who cares?
No one does,

They all got their own shit of life priorities,
And whether you like it or not,
You're not the first.
But you know who's gonna put you first?
You. Yourself.
Put your full name here because,
It's the one who's gonna always put you first.

So whether they care or not ,
You shouldn't care,
Because the most important person on earth,
Will always care.

You will always care,
For yourself
Until they get disturbed.

Shallow

So shallow,
So disgusting,
How they assume,
That I'm pretending.

So weird;
So disappointing,
How they assume:
That I'm faking.

All the hard work,
The smiles,
And energy was seen,
As seeking for—
Validation.

If my real face seems fake,
Then I got nothing to say,
But they are—
Shallow.

Courage

Bright green, yellow and red.
Bright me on the bed,
Near me close I'm fed,
Hear me alone I led,
Fear me away I fled,
Bright green, yellow and red.

Pearl Rotana

Blue oceans green trees,
Grey streets white fields,
High buildings orange suits,
Yellow vests grey shoes,
White cars and buses,
Circular and cubix,
Blue oceans green trees,
My favorite nature feeds.

Purpose

I seize opportunities, not sacrifice them,
I care for myself, not hate it,
I live to heal not to exaggerate,
I write to inspire yes, but also,
To make it—as a poet.

Ingram Content Group UK Ltd.
Milton Keynes UK
UKHW021055120323
418388UK00012B/145